LOVE YOUR TEENS...
THEY'LL LOVE YOU BACK!

A Simple Guide To
Enjoying Your Teenagers

By
Inger Lundgren Schmutz

Love Your Teens... They'll Love You Back! A Simple Guide to Enjoying Your Teenagers©

Copyright ©2004 by Creative Publishing

Published by:
Creative Publishing
2221 Justin Road #119-123
Flower Mound, Texas 75028

Send all requests for information to the above address.

Printed in the United States of America

TABLE OF CONTENTS

ABOUT THE AUTHOR

I have been married for over 37 years to the most wonderful and kind man I have ever known. He is brilliant, giving, stalwart, frugal, talented, funny, dedicated, sweet-natured, patriotic, and he can do story problems and solve riddles! My life really began when I married him. I have been blessed greater than anyone could imagine, with five children who are abundantly talented, each in their own individual ways, but one thing they all have in common is their value systems. My children are kind, caring, thoughtful individuals. Jennifer, Kassandra, Melanie, Sterling and Stephanie.

I believe that I have been able to make the biggest difference in others' lives by being a homemaker. I believe that we all impact other people's lives in one way or another; however, I have had the opportunity to impact 5 persons (my kids) and my husband as well, by trying to be a good mom and wife and homemaker, and it was all GREAT FUN! While I enjoyed completing my Bachelors of Science Degree in Behavioral Sciences, I would definitely choose being a mother at home as my favorite career.

The years of my life have been so wonderful, that truly, I would like to live them all over again! While I have had my share of trials, I have been so blessed with family, health, happiness, prosperity, freedom, travel, autonomy, and wonderful experiences. The things in my life that I believe to be "successes" are the obstacles that I have overcome, the values that I have learned, the faith that I have been able to muster, the gratitude that I have learned to feel, and the knowledge that I have been able to attain in all aspects of life. If there is anything I would change about my life, it would be this ... I would like to have MORE time with my husband, MORE time with my children, MORE time to think and ponder, MORE time to serve, and MORE willingness to be giving and selfless.

INTRODUCTION

When first-time parents leave the hospital with their brand new baby, payment of the bill is all that is required to check out. No one solicits "parent credentials," no tests are given, and no child-rearing manuals are distributed. We must figure it out on our own. From birth through early childhood, on to the teenage years, and into adulthood, we have to learn how to interact with our offspring.

I've heard people joke that they were wonderful parents until they had their first child. Most of us do want to be good parents; but parenting does not come naturally for everyone. Individuals are not even required to be licensed for this arduous task. In most vocations, training, permits, degrees and preparation are necessary; but for the most important job of all, no training whatsoever is required.

My purpose in writing this book is simply this: to convey what I have learned from raising five children, and to comment on what I have observed in others. Parenting does necessitate the development of skills; however, for the most part, parents can be successful by heeding this simple truth:

"Love your teenagers,
and they'll love you back!"

CHAPTER 1
NURTURING FRIENDSHIPS

"The greatest use of life is to spend it for
something that will outlast it."
- William James

Some contend that parents should not "be friends" with their children—I disagree. On the contrary, parents should become best friends with their children.

Throughout life, people develop and nurture friendships. As George Washington once said, "Friendship is a plant of slow growth." When a person decides to make a new friend, there is a set of social norms—a checklist, if you will—that we go through to develop that friendship. That same friendship is attainable with our children.

Since you are reading this book, you must have the desire to develop a better relationship with your teen. Desire is the first step. Once you have made the choice to become better friends with your teen, the next step is to take action. Employ the same principles with your teenager that you use when developing a new friendship with a complete stranger. The following principles will be helpful in developing new friendships with your teens—and, anyone else, for that matter.

Be Interested

Dale Carnegie said, "you can make more friends in two months by becoming really interested in other people than you can in two years by trying to get other people interested in you."

In order to make new friends, we must be interested in them. Have you heard the saying, "If you're interested, you're interesting!"? The corollary is also true: "To be interesting, you must be interested!"

If a friend asks you a question and only pauses briefly to let you answer, you would think that your friend is not really interested in what you have to say. The next time your friend asks you a question, you'll most likely give them a surface answer, knowing they're not listening anyway.

Our teens are the same. In fact, they need more assurance that we are genuinely interested and attentively listening. Only then will they feel the desire to share more with us. Develop an interest in even the mundane details of their daily lives. They will be more apt to listen to what parents have to say if parents listen first.

Be Non-judgmental

God, Himself, doesn't judge man until the end of his days... why should we?

Think back to the last time someone assumed something about you or labeled you. Maybe you overheard a conversation at the office. You probably didn't feel that the label fit you. In our society, adolescents suffer from preconceived notions regarding what they as a group are like. When we proceed from prejudice, we take a possibility and turn it into a reality. Suspend all labels when it comes to *your* teenager. Give them the opportunity to prove themselves.

Give children a safe environment to make mistakes without criticism. Show empathy—express confidence in their ability to make good decisions, or to make better decisions the next time. In this way, situations can become a platform for discussion rather than criticism.

Enjoy Activities With Them

My best advice for parents and their teenagers can be summed up in three simple words: hang with them! Order a pizza and hang out, just like you would with your peers.

A friend once complained that he didn't know what to do with his struggling teenage son. I asked what his son's interests were, to which he replied, "All he ever does is skateboard." So I suggested that he take his son to a skateboard park to spend some time with him. He exhaustedly replied that that would drive him nuts. This father will never become close to his son with this type of attitude.

Give Them Space and Respect

I read about a mother who was frustrated with her teenager's dirty room, so she threw the contents of her daughter's room out the window onto the lawn for all to see. While she thought she was teaching her daughter a lesson... her daughter only saw how little her mother respected her, her belongings, and her privacy.

When we demonstrate to our teens that we trust and respect them, they will want to reciprocate.

Be Patient

Although we may disagree with some of their choices, chances are that with our peers, we are very tactful when we bring up our differences. Why not extend the same courtesy to our children, and have patience with their choices?

Develop Common Interests

We do this with our peers... attend book clubs, join bowling leagues, sing in a choir. If your child expresses a desire to learn a new skill (karate, art, etc.), consider taking the class with them.

Be Flexible

When we are willing to change, we communicate to our teens that it's OK for them to do the same. Very few things are set in stone, and even if relationships have become negative, human beings can change. In fact, life is a series of changes in feelings, attitudes, behaviors and beliefs. Relationships can always be improved. "A bend in the road isn't the end of the road, unless you fail to make the turn!" (*Successories Series*)

Never Use Sarcasm

Sarcasm should *not ever* be a mode of communication with teens. It is the lowest form of humor. It is unnecessary, insidious, ineffective, and demolishes self-confidence. Parents who resort to sarcasm usually lack self-confidence themselves.

Why aren't we best friends with our teenagers? I've come up with two likely reasons. The first is that we are familiar with our own kids. We, therefore, don't try to use our best manners and most courteous and disciplined behavior in getting along with them. The second is that many parents think that their *only* role is that they must teach their kids.

As Dr. Stephen R. Covey explains, first, our children watch our example. Then we're able to build a relationship with them. Only after we have built that relationship can we teach them. Many parents try to teach before a relationship is established... it just won't work. Of course we should be teaching our kids, but not by preaching, lecturing, demanding, ridiculing, or threatening. We must teach through example, love, and friendship.

Gordon B. Hinckley, a religious leader, once counseled parents: "Be kind to your children. Be companionable with them. Every child is entitled to grow up in a home where there is warm and secure companionship, where there is love in family relationships, where appreciation for one another is taught and exemplified."

There are those parents who view their children as excess baggage -- they are always looking for ways to free themselves of the responsibility they have to spend time with them. How sad!

We usually treat our friends very well, but our own children don't always see our best. The familiar scenario is one we all know... parents scream at their kids, and yet when the phone rings, they answer with an ever-so-pleasant "Hello." This must be very annoying to our children.

Susan Hansen, author and mother of a four-year-old, heard a knock at the door and went to answer it. Standing there was her small son. She said "Hi John." He replied, "Hi Mom. I just wanted to see your company face." What a wake-up call. The place we need to smile most is at home.

Teenagers should be treated just as we would like them to treat us: with trust, loyalty, love, and respect. It is simply stated in the Golden Rule, "Do unto others as you would have others do unto you." This means that you love them enough to give them respect, to listen to them with trust, and to be loyal to them. Understand that they are not yet adults and that they are dealing with peer pressure as well as physical changes. Give your teens an abundance of praise. Look for positive things that you can comment upon, no matter how small. This praise must be genuine and heart-felt. It is certain that even young children, and especially teenagers, can see through pretense. Praise them every day. Hold them, hug and squeeze them, and tell them they are irresistible, handsome, and beautiful. Compliment them when you pick them up after school by saying something like "I sure am lucky to have you!" It is critical that parents focus on finding the positives in their teenagers. If we always seek negatives, we will certainly find them; however, if we begin looking for and pointing out the positives, we will begin to find more of them.

When teenagers hear their parents praise them as their parents are talking to others, they will try to live up to the expectations implied in the praises. One woman said, "When I was a teenager, I heard my mom say to her friends that she could have ten kids if they were all like me." The woman always remembered that compliment and felt pride and respect for her mom and dad. Because of her parents' respect for her, she never wanted to do anything to break that trust. She did not lie to them or deceive them, and thus she promoted their continued respect and love.

In contrast to this woman's experience, once while in a doctor's office, I overheard a mother say to the receptionist, in front of her teenage son, "I can't wait till Eric is eighteen so I can kick him out of the house and my husband and I can go play." Eric appeared to be dismayed about her comments. What a world of difference parental attitude can make in a teenager's behavior.

What do you do when you are in love with someone? You tell them that they are beautiful, smart, handsome, and wonderful. We should be eager to show the same attention to our children. They need to know that we love them, and telling them frequently is the only way they will know. Tell your teenagers you are glad that God sent them to you. Think back to your courting days and replicate some of those silly, young, fun things you did:

IDEAS:

❧   Leave sweet notes in lunches

❧   Take your teens out on dates

❧   Bring them breakfast in bed (My husband used to cook our kids ebelskivers – puffy, sphere-shaped Scandinavian pancakes… they usually ended up playing ball with the leftovers)

- Play hooky from work and school and go build sandcastles on the beach
- Go people-watching at a public place
- Write a cute message on their bathroom mirror with lipstick
- Run in the rain in your swimsuits (One of my favorite memories is when three of my teens pulled me out into the front yard during a rainstorm to jump in the puddles with them!)
- Volunteer at a homeless shelter together
- Attend a lecture/speaker then go discuss what you both thought of it over ice-cream cones
- Read a book together
- Give a homemade book of 'coupons' (Good for 1 banana split; Good for 1 week of no chores; Freebie – you choose; etc.)
- Stay up until 2AM Friday night watching a movie of their choice

- Attend their extracurricular events and be their best cheerleader
- Call their cell phone and leave them a message—be creative
- Get a manicure and/or pedicure together

I know of one father who surprised his son by picking him up from school and flying with him to one of his business meetings. They spent the day together, and the son, 25 years later, still recollects how important it made him feel that his father would include him in his day-to-day schedule.

To love your children also means to be loyal to them. Don't talk behind their back; don't joke about them or about teenagers in general. As a parent, do you enjoy it when your kids talk negatively about you to their friends? I often hear disparaging remarks about parents from high school kids. In our family, we have never wanted our kids to call us "Sir" or "Ma'am" because we don't think it is conducive to friendship. I know many parents who demand that their kids refer to them in this formal manner, but good friends do not refer to each other in this way. If only the parents had a clue about how their kids really refer to them behind their backs!   Don't get me wrong – it's important that teens have a healthy respect for authority, but that comes from building a relationship one step at a time. In a community bulletin I once saw this announcement: "Take an adult bus trip ... what a great way to get away from your kids during Spring Break." Parents would not be happy if organized youth groups encouraged trips for the purpose of teens getting away from their parents! Remember: It is never too late to love your teenager. My advice is simple: Be best friends with them.

CHAPTER 2
TIME AND FUN

"You rarely succeed
unless you have fun doing it."
-Anonymous

Play

Have you heard the cliché, "Families who pray together, stay together?" I propose another cliché, which has been just as true for our family: families that **_PLAY_** together stay together. People love to have fun, and families need to have fun together.

Interestingly, this same philosophy is prevalent in the education field as well. I listened to an educator speak on television once. He very aptly said: "The key to education is to make it FUN, especially math and science classes."

Learning can happen even when we're having a good time. We lose teens to their peers because generally they have more fun with their friends than they do with their families. It is my position that when children play and have fun within the family, a major need has been satisfied. If at a young age they are content and having fun, they will be content in the boundaries of their own families. Play with your kids and spend time with them because you *want* to, not because you *have* to…your kids know the difference.

This principle is exemplified by a family who used to live next door to us. The mother and father of four could usually be seen outside playing ball, roller-skating, bike riding, or at the pool swimming together. They laugh with their children and enjoy being with them. It is obvious to their children and to observers alike that their children are their first priority. Joe E. Lewis wisely said, "you only live once, but if you work it right, once is enough."

Motivation

Do you want your teenagers to *want* to attend school or church? Try making it fun! I spent an afternoon with a mother and daughter who bickered and called each other names. They disagreed about a simple issue. The daughter didn't like school and the mother forced her without question. I imagined what could have happened if the mother had gone beyond the superficial, and dug down deeper to get at the root of the problem. Perhaps the mother could pick her daughter up from school, rather than have her ride the bus, and go for a walk or get a treat as they discussed the day's events. The important thing the mother should grasp is that if her daughter understands why she goes to school and participates in its surrounding activities, she will enjoy it more, and will be more motivated.

One father helped his daughter in middle school when she was frantic and very unhappy about the prospects of writing a report about Japan. He began to bring up trivia in their conversations about Japan and its people. Then he offered to help her with the report. They decided to draw a Japanese woman on the cover and then dress her in real fabric pieces. The result was a beautiful cover and an interesting report. From then on, this young lady was excited to write reports because her father had taken the time to show her how interesting and fun it can be.

Religious leader David O. McKay once said, "No other success can compensate for failure in the home." So, do the "work" which awaits you at home, and have fun while you do it. Enjoy your teens just as you enjoy your friends.

<u>Quality versus Quantity</u>

God did not give us our children for only when they fit into our schedule. He gave them to us for always. They are here, whether we make time for them, or not. I believe the term "quality time" is a cop-out for parents. There must be both quality and quantity. A parent must be available for the teaching moment when it arises, which may or may not happen during a scheduled "quality time." Parents who value their kids enough to spend large quantities of time with them will teach their children that they are valuable to the parents. Thus, the children will be more likely to value themselves. Teenagers need to know that they are very high on their parents' priority list and that their parents like them enough to spend lots of time with them.

It is difficult to create quality time—it usually happens spontaneously. We can plan events and hope that they will be uplifting, enriching, or fun, but it won't always happen. Often, things will go wrong, someone is in a bad mood, or other activities conflict.

For instance, for years our family had planned a special vacation to a historical spot in which we were very interested. We finally made it to this spectacular place with video camera in hand. Because we had been camping in the heat and humidity for the previous two weeks, it was only natural that most of us were grumpy. What we expected to be the utmost quality experience turned out to be the very opposite. The kids pouted and argued and we were all quite annoyed with each other. After the vacation, we talked about erasing the video in the hopes that on another trip we could have a better, "quality" experience. We never got around to erasing it, which was fortunate; now we turn it on occasionally for a good laugh.

I had a college professor who shared her heartbreaking story with our class. She said that as a mother of three young children, she always felt like a nobody. She decided that she needed to "make something of herself." So she enrolled in school and after many years earned her Ph.D. Tears filled her eyes as she told us she realized that her degree didn't make her a 'somebody' any more than did being the mother of those sweet children. In fact, she had missed out on her children's childhoods by always being in school. She could never bring back those years and could never relive the experiences she missed with them. Although this story is disheartening, it is a good reminder that it is never too late to begin to build relationships, even with adult children. It is never too late to make new friendships.

Years ago I read an impressive story about a father who was very involved with his daughter and her friends. The girl's friends often teased her about how he always had to know where she was and when she would be coming home. One evening, when the daughter was in high school, she and her friends went out. Naturally, her father wanted to know all the details, including what time she would be home and which highway they would be driving on. Late that night on the girls' way home, they encountered a dangerous blizzard. Their car stalled and they were trapped in the deep snowdrifts. As they pondered their frightening predicament, one of the girl's friends said, "Don't worry, your Dad will be here soon." Sure enough, minutes later they saw headlights on the desolate highway - - it was her father. It was not the girl's peers that came looking for her, but a loving father. *Be* that loving parent.

Priorities

I like something Anne Dillard said, "how we spend our days, is, of course, how we spend our lives." People make time to do the things they really desire to do. I was impressed with two anonymous quotes I heard while taking the Franklin Covey Day Planner course: "We all have all the time there is," and "What we believe in, we have time for." Hence, it all depends on how we set our priorities. It's what we make time for that counts. Make time for your teen.

Since we chose to bring children into this world, they are our responsibility. They should be our focus. Make time for them first, after your spouse. If you put your children first, chances are they will put you first. If you are loyal to your children, then they will be loyal to you, and feel close to you. Put in the effort now so that you can enjoy them when they get older.

Effective parenting can be narrowed down to two words: TIME and FUN. This is what it takes.

CHAPTER 3
COMMUNICATION

"Your worst enemies are made when you ignore people. Those boys... who shot classmates, didn't do that because they woke up with a positive self image that morning... No, they felt ignored, rejected, humiliated, and wanted revenge."
-Tori Amos

Be Available

This means at all times... twenty-four hours a day, seven days a week. Believe it or not, I know parents who will not accept phone calls after 10:30PM from anyone, including their own children. Make certain your teenagers know they can reach you <u>at any time</u> to talk. Allow your teenager to have your complete attention. You can talk, laugh, sing, and analyze friends and situations. You would be surprised at how many deep personal thoughts can emerge at unexpected hours. Be available to talk when your teen is ready to talk. All of my five adult children have expressed gratitude that one or both of their parents always waited up for them to come home from dates or parties so they could share what happened, and could talk about their feelings and thoughts.

One mother of five teenagers said that her 16-year-old daughter's talkative time is after 10:00PM. But since the mother is too tired to talk at that time, she rolls over in bed and pretends to be asleep when the daughter comes in after dates or activities. That way she knows she won't be up until midnight listening to her teenage daughter. It makes me sad when I think of all the important dialoguing experiences that this mother missed out on because she prioritized sleep over building a lasting relationship with her child.

Make Time

Dialogue takes time. It is the key to relationships with others, not only with parent-child relationships, but with spousal relationships as well. This dialogue must be in the form of conversations: talking and listening, rather than ordering, threatening or bossing. Talk about current events, friends, situations, social issues, religious topics—whatever you would talk to your friends about. Through dialogue with teenagers, eventually the values of parents and teens begin to coincide more and more because current issues and problems are being discussed. This brings me to my next point...

Role-play

One of our favorite times as a family was waiting for one of the kids to come home from a date. The siblings couldn't wait to participate in what we call Role-play. We have some fond memories of watching our children act out how their date tried to hold their hand, or steal a kiss, or how close they wanted to dance. Role-playing can and should be used in *all* scenarios—we role-play everything:

- Telephone manners
- How to meet people (Do you ever cringe when you see your teen meet someone, and they don't even make eye contact?)
- 'What If?' situations ('What if someone asked you to smoke with them…what would you do?')

We learn by doing. Put a jar on the dinner table titled, "Information Station," with slips of paper, each having different topics, questions or ideas. Discuss them during dinner, and then act them out.

Be Understanding

Help your kids learn to understand their own behavior as well as that of others. This is done through communication. When your own behavior is unacceptable, give your kids the rationale behind your moods or unseemly behavior. They will be more sympathetic towards you, and will know that you also have trying times. They have the capacity to support us and empathize with us as their parents, and they will, if given the opportunity.

Be Approachable

I once observed a teenage boy at a dance with his friends. When he noticed his mother enter the room, he left his circle of peers and threw his arms around her. His face was beaming as he kissed her and cheerfully whispered, "I just wanted to say I love you." Because of the open lines of communication already established, it was easy for this young man to express himself to his mother without any hesitation.

Take joy in being a parent! Enjoy the uniqueness of your child, and remember: be the kind of parent that your teen will look at and think, "I sure got a good deal."

Physical Contact

Teenagers need physical contact. A study was conducted during wartime in Europe involving orphanages. The infants were given all the food and physical care they needed, but due to lack of personnel, were never held, cuddled, or loved. They all died. Our kids are with us for such a short time. Let's take advantage of the time we have to be friends with them in our own homes and not let time go by when we have not hugged and praised our kids. Kids need our unconditional love.

Share

Share family information with your teenagers. This does three things: builds trust, teaches them responsibility, and teaches them problem-solving skills. In our family, financial matters are openly discussed with our teenagers, along with other personal information because we trust them implicitly. Being completely open with them also teaches them to handle private matters pertaining to the family in a responsible manner; however, I do not encourage dwelling on depressing issues. These topics can be discussed in a way that teaches teens how to take positive action to deal with these situations. In other words, teenagers have many problems of their own and we need not burden them unnecessarily. However, they should participate in discussing family issues that will ultimately aid in family unity. For example, when discussing salary, ask for their help to outline a budget: plan a menu, shop together, and try to stick to it. This can help them develop financial skills, while it also gets the family together.

Give Rationale

A science teacher gives students a reason for combining certain chemicals to produce particular results. In time, students learn to trust the teacher's judgment so that when he forbids them from combining certain chemicals to safeguard against a dangerous reaction, they'll respond immediately.

An important part of clear communication is providing plenty of rationale in advance, when you are giving instructions to your children. They like to know why. Explain why you are asking certain things of them, and they will respond more positively. Begin with positive statements and then give explanations and reasons. Don't be selfish and domineering by saying, "Because I said so." When they understand the logic behind your instructions, they will be more willing to comply. Then, when occasionally you may need to ask something of them without giving rationale, they will trust you and do it more willingly.

And don't forget tangible rewards—they really work! Let them know that by choosing actions, they have also chosen the consequences. Acting appropriately brings rewards and freedom; the converse is also true.

Teach them to adhere to their values and principles. Hopefully, values are the reasons for doing things. If you and your teen agree on your value structure, then many things won't even be issues, because they will govern themselves. We establish value systems by being best friends with our teenagers, and by living up to those principles, ourselves. Ultimately, rationale for value systems will enable them to become upright citizens and honorable adults.

Be A Good Negotiator

It is important to become a good negotiator, which means to seek consensus, to barter, and to compromise. There are times when this is necessary. How often do we say "no" to our teens' requests simply because it would inconvenience us? Is it really bad to let them go to their friend's house, or is it possible that we are just too tired to drive them there? Dialogue to find the best solutions that work for your family, and above all, be flexible.

CHAPTER 4
ACKNOWLEDGE FEELINGS

"Feelings are real and legitimate;
Children behave and misbehave for a reason, even if
adults can not figure it out"
- Anonymous

Acknowledge the feelings of your teenagers. Nothing is more irritating than not being understood or heard. Each one of us is entitled to have our feelings and to express them. We must accept the fact that our children's feelings exist. Encouraging your teens to express their feelings is good, but don't try to force them to stop feeling them. Sometimes what our feelings cause us to do may be wrong, but the feelings, in and of themselves, are a natural thing. Show them that you can be a good listener. Ask questions to ensure you have a good understanding of their viewpoint.

In a dentist's office, I once overheard a woman demonstrate one of the most vivid examples of a parent not acknowledging feelings that I have ever seen. While waiting in the dentist's office one day, I observed a mother with a child. The child told his mother "Mom, I want to go to McDonalds today." The mother replied, "No you don't, now stop talking about it, we're not going." It was very interesting to see the behavior of the boy in response to his mother's failure to acknowledge his feelings. He became very boisterous and rude, and began to tear pages out of a book. The mother yelled at him, told him he was bad, and said that she was going to spank him.

Imagine that the mother had been with a friend or associate - and this person had said they wanted to go to McDonalds. Do you think for a minute she would have responded with, "No you don't"? If only she had given her child the courtesy of acknowledging his feelings, then this situation might have been avoided. This does not mean she had to give in to him. A better response to this child would have been, "So you want to go to McDonalds? Well, I can understand that because we always have such a good time there, and I know you like their food; but, today it won't be convenient to go to McDonalds. We'll try to go soon." Through years of being a consistent listener, you'll evoke a better response from teens. Start while they're young to listen and acknowledge their feelings.

It has been said that adolescence is a period of storm and stress. Conversely, adolescence is also a time of achievement and development in all aspects. Many teens that I have spoken with and observed say that the reason they don't get into trouble and are able to enjoy their teenage years is because their energies are devoted to dance, music, volunteer work, sports, church, studies, clubs, and other hobbies that encourage their development. These activities also develop self-esteem, which is vital to teens. Avoid going to the opposite extreme by enrolling them in too many things – avoid burn out. Balance is the key.

We must be tuned in during this crucial time of shifting moods and thought patterns. If we acknowledge their feelings, they'll learn to do the same with themselves and others. This will promote a healthy cycle. I once read an article by a doctor who specializes in rearing children. He said that the two most important things to remember when you are parenting are: be tender, and be available. What great advice! Tenderness and availability are key elements in our relationships with everyone—particularly our teenagers.

Thus, it is important that we not only listen closely, but also actually hear what our teens have to say. In acknowledging their feelings, realize that they may think differently than we did as teenagers, and do as adults.

Society is very different now, and so are the pressures. Support them, listen to them, and acknowledge how they feel. You may be surprised at the reaction you will get.

CHAPTER 5
<u>MEETING NEEDS</u>

"When we, as parents, show caring
and love in meeting our children's needs,
we help our children grow up to be
strong and caring people."
-H. Wallace Goddard

Parents must make every effort to ascertain the needs of their children, and then attempt to meet them. I have heard parents of wayward children say, "I taught them the right things and now they are making bad choices on their own." Perhaps this is an easy way out. As parents, we need to ask ourselves every day if we are meeting the needs of our children: do we give a higher priority to work or other activities? Too many parents send their kids to church, youth night, and school functions, expecting that these institutions will close the gap that they as parents are leaving open. However, they choose not to be directly and actively involved with their children. These same parents still believe that they have fulfilled their parental responsibilities. I have also known parents who place blame on church leaders, schoolteachers, or friends for their own shortcomings as parents.

The common excuse, "When we moved to a new city, the kids didn't adjust because they missed their friends" is sad. If family is their primary group rather than peers, then the adjustment will be easier. Parents fail to understand that although shuffling kids to church, school, and other activities is worthwhile, it does not, in and of itself, constitute good parenting. We, as parents, must meet our children's needs. Put the effort into your children now, and the payback is immeasurable later.

Teenagers need lots of *attention*, *protection,* and *rest*. They usually fall short on all three. Help them as much as possible through dialogue and setting some limits. Their needs will involve a time commitment. Instructions cannot merely be dealt to kids. They must be influenced by loving parents who are involved on a daily basis because they want to be, and who spend a great deal of time with their kids. Again, quality and quantity are essential. The key is LOTS OF TIME.

Pay Attention

Off and on throughout the years, I was a substitute teacher at the high school where my children attended school. On several occasions, I asked teenagers questions about their relationships with their parents. Most responses were similar to these:

☹ "My Dad is counting down the days 'til I'm gone"

☹ "My parents would rather me lie to them about where I've been than to tell them the truth about a party"

☹ "I will not tell my parents *anything*, because they yell uncontrollably, so... I lie instead"

☹ "I hate my parents"

☹ "I'd tell them more things if they'd just be cool about it"

☹ "I love my Dad, but he forces me to do what HE wants"

If the parents of these teens were attempting to meet their needs, then these teenagers would probably not be expressing these particular feelings.

A newspaper told of a twelve-year-old boy who shot himself and one other person to death because he was distraught about an extra-credit homework assignment that his parents wanted him to do. The question must be asked: Why did he do this? His death was so unnecessary. How could this have been avoided? One way would have been to engage him in dialogue. Perhaps the parents could have prevented his suicide if they had talked with him more about his pressures. Furthermore, they could have helped him with his extra-credit project and made it fun for him, rather than overwhelming. Maybe they could have given him a tangible reward. Without knowing full details of this particular situation, it seems that this young man's needs could have been better identified and more adeptly addressed by his parents.

Identify Needs

Each person is totally unique, with their own puzzle that needs to be solved in order to discover exactly what their particular needs are. One child's needs are not necessarily those of another. Parents who say they have taken care of their children's needs by treating them all exactly the same are making a mistake.

Give each child separate and individual time to be with you alone. Go out to lunch. Allow them to skip school on their birthday and spend the day together doing what interests them. My son's birthday is in the summer, so we allowed him to choose a school day to celebrate. We simply wrote a note to the school explaining what we were allowing him to do. One of my daughters has a birthday that usually falls on Thanksgiving weekend, so she also selects another school day to celebrate alone with her parents. Find special things that only you and your child can do, thus creating a bond between parent and child. The stronger this bond, the easier it will be to identify and subsequently begin to meet their needs.

I remember being in a friend's home one day when her 13-year-old son came in from the school bus. He was noticeably angry and immediately began to hit and yell at his younger siblings. In turn, he was yelled at and sent to his room. After a few moments I walked into his room and sat down next to him. I began making conversation and asking about his day. I discovered that on the school bus on his way home, other youngsters had taken his prize science project and completely destroyed it. So, there was a viable explanation for his behavior. If his parents had met his needs by noticing the change in his behavior and dialoguing with him rather than giving strict punishment, the situation could have been handled more positively.

One of the most important things we can do as parents for children is to be certain that they can always be 'authentic' or 'real' with us. In other words, we don't want our children to have to hide who they really are or their feelings from us. That means—you guessed it – lots of dialogue and acceptance of their feelings. When they can't be 'real,' they are more prone to being depressed, lonely, or stressed.

Protect Them

Another need that our teenagers have is to be protected. They need to have you be on their side - always. Send notes to your kid's teachers and school administrators expressing gratitude and support as well as other concerns you may have. Love your kids enough to fiercely protect them from schoolteachers and administrators who might be unfair, especially in the elementary grades. Your kids, their teachers, and their administrators need to know that you are completely aware of what is happening at school. Don't be afraid to negotiate with teachers and administrators. Always let your kids know that you are supportive of them.

You can support their teachers and at the same time, make certain they are being appropriate with your kids in the classroom.

A social worker who was an administrator for a teenage boy's home told me about a very disheartening experience. One of the boys had a court date and the judge had requested the presence of the boy's father. In my estimation, this was most definitely a need that the father should have fulfilled. When the social worker called the father, who was an active member of church and community, the father said he could not be present because of a church activity that particular day. Clearly, the father had long ago stopped trying to meet his son's needs.

A certain way to make sure that you do not meet your teenager's needs is to kick them out of their home. I have talked to many teenagers who have been told by their parents to "get out." Barring extreme cases and extenuating circumstances, parents who force their children out have not been successful in identifying and meeting their children's needs, or in trying to, have become frustrated. Kicking them out might remove the problem from your immediate view, but will not resolve the conflict.

Help Them Rest

Provide "unstructured time" when they can be restful. A woman once told me, "I can't wait for summer—I already have my children's summer schedule made out." She had typing classes, gymnastics, lessons of every kind, and activities filling up each day. Rather than filling up their time for them, ask them how they would like to spend their time. Be certain to include lots of family fun times, such as vacations, weekend getaways, late movie nights with pizza, staying up late to talk, or kidnap your kids occasionally for an overnighter.

Use caution in believing that teenagers need to work during the school year, or even during the summer. Their 'work' is being done if they are trying hard in school and participating in extra-curricular activities. They have the rest of their lives to have jobs. I have seen many parents throughout the years who force their children to get jobs to teach them responsibility. I believe that they will learn responsibility through their schoolwork and activities, as well as gain and develop invaluable skills and knowledge. Don't force them to carry the burden of choosing between finishing homework and getting to their job on time. It is our responsibility as parents to provide for our children's *basic needs*. They can be responsible for their extra *wants*. They will become responsible if parents set a responsible example and are responsible people.

CHAPTER 6
COMPETING WITH PEERS

"When we ask which person in our lives means the most to us, we often find that it is those who, instead of giving much advice, solutions, or cures, have chosen rather to share our pain and touch our wounds with a gentle and tender hand. The friend who can be silent with us in a moment of despair or confusion, who can stay with us in an hour of grief and bereavement, who can tolerate not knowing, not curing, not healing and face with us the reality of our powerlessness, that is a friend who cares."
-Henri Nouwen

Make it a point to compete with your children's peers. There are three areas in which peers fulfill each other's needs. These are (1) fun activities, (2) questions about intimacy, and (3) open dialogue. If parents and families can provide these three elements for each other, then negative peer pressure is greatly reduced.

Fun Activities

It requires effort to compete with peers. If your kids are invited to an activity that is questionable, then come up with a more exciting plan. Our daughter was once invited to a beach party that we didn't want her to attend. In order to compete with her peers, we planned an overnight excursion to a local hotel with swimming, tennis, workout room, steam and sauna. This alternative activity provided the family with a wonderful time together, and my daughter repeatedly thanked us for providing such a fun evening.

Date your children - one on one. Our children have shared with us that some of their best childhood memories were of our dates with them. Our children enjoyed going to see Jaws 3-D with Mom; going to The Nutcracker with Dad. The excuse that there is no money for family fun doesn't always hold true. For years people have said to me, "We don't have money for vacations with the family." These same people seem to have funds for many other things that are non-essential. I knew a man who had seven children. He claimed he had no time or money for family vacations. He was, however, able to purchase for himself an expensive telescope, and other items that were of no interest to the rest of his family. It all depends on where we place our priorities. Not everything costs money. Look for free community events. The local library and City Hall are an excellent resource for ideas. Show them a good time, but don't overindulge them—keep good boundaries. Dating your teens will bring you closer together and strengthen your relationship.

Questions About Intimacy

Let your teen bring up any topic. During a date with one of my children, my teen brought up a specific and sensitive, sexual topic. We proceeded to have a lengthy conversation, during which I shared the facts that I knew, some statistics, and also my personal values with reference to it. I was very pleased that my teen chose not to discuss this topic with friends but rather with me, and I expressed my appreciation that they would feel comfortable enough and trusted me enough to bring up the subject.

Among their peers, most kids laugh and joke about sexual issues. Isn't it better that we provide a comfortable atmosphere in the home, which will facilitate accurate awareness and respect for this important topic?

Be open and approachable; parents are the ones who can set the example of showing respect for the body as well as its functions, and at the same time they can be willing and unembarrassed to discuss all aspects of sexuality in the home. If you have a difficult time talking about the topic of physical intimacy, practice aloud in front of the mirror, or with a friend or spouse. This will allow you to overcome the potential awkwardness so that you can be prepared and comfortable when talking with your teen.

<u>Open Dialogue</u>

A teenager's feelings are validated by their peers. We can give them this same support by not talking down to them or being condescending. Peers don't "boss" each other -- why should we? We can use ways to communicate wherein we build self-esteem rather than destroy it.

Be there to talk about anything that's on their mind. There are no topics that are off-limits. Our kids can and should be able to ask us anything, and know that we will respond calmly and in a manner that validates their question. If we don't provide this outlet for them, they will most certainly turn to their peers. When that happens, parents will have lost the opportunity to teach true principles.

A young woman approached her father to broach the topic of sex. She said, "Dad, I know about oral sex." His response was, "Who told you about that?" When she said her friends told her, he merely kept a straight face, and walked away. Who do you think this daughter will choose to confide in next time she has a topic she wants to talk about? Certainly, not her father.

When our children come to us, we need to be ready, willing, and *interested* in what they have to say. Oftentimes people claim that they were not raised in a home with parents who fostered open conversation about such topics, and they are therefore not comfortable discussing it with their children. Although this may be the case, those parents are merely continuing a cycle which may lead to detrimental consequences. Children who can't talk to their parents *will* go elsewhere. First, they'll be seeking conversation, then comfort, then maybe more. Show them from the beginning that anything is fair game to talk about in the home.

CHAPTER 7
CONFLICT RESOLUTION

*"I argue very well. Ask any of my remaining friends.
I can win an argument on any topic, against any
opponent. People know this, and steer clear of me at
parties. Often, as a sign of their great respect,
they don't even invite me."*
-Dave Barry

It's insightful to take a course in human relations. These classes enable you to role-play situations, and obtain helpful feedback. As was described earlier, role-playing helps us learn skills properly through practice. These are skills that all human beings need.

The three main things to remember in conflict resolution are (1) active listening, (2) "I"-messages, and (3) non-judgmental response.

Active listening

Listen not only to words, but also to feelings and non-verbal messages (body language), and then address all of those things in your response. It is interesting to note that the word 'listen' has the same letters as the word 'silent.'

"I"–Messages

In order to say how you feel without making the other person feel like they are being put down, use an "I"-message. For example: "I worry and feel sad when it gets late and I have not heard from you." This is better than saying "You are so irresponsible and lazy; you can't even take the time to call home." Using "I"-messages takes practice and concentration, but what a difference it makes in the response you will get from your teen.

Non-Judgmental Response

No matter what, avoid an angry confrontation. Listen to your children just as you would listen to a friend. Normally you would commiserate and express understanding and support, rather than criticize and provoke an argument. Do the same with your teen.

All of us need to blow off steam occasionally and just need to be heard. If your kids tell you something totally shocking, restrain yourself, be calm, and just listen. You may even have to wait a couple of days and then say to them, "You know, I've been thinking about what you said the other day, and I wanted to share some thoughts that I had about that."

If your children are sad or depressed, don't let them sulk in their rooms alone for long periods of time. Go in and sit with them. Just be available and *quiet.* Comfort them; provide a safe haven for your teenager... it is our #1 responsibility.

Sometimes your teen may not be ready to share information with you because of prior negative experiences or other reasons. Continue listening to their feelings and their tone of voice and observing their body language; give feedback on what you are hearing. Be diligent: keep listening until your kids want to share information with you. If you are a true friend to them, they will eventually want to share their burdens with you, just as a good friend would.

For years, we as parents have been resolving conflicts in one way or another. Whether or not we teach our offspring to resolve problems effectively depends on our approach. So be aware that your children are watching your every move. Try to consistently resolve conflicts in an equitable manner.

CHAPTER 8
<u>CONSEQUENCES</u>

*"I believe that we are solely responsible for
our choices, and we have to accept the
consequences of every deed, word,
and thought throughout our lifetime."*
-Elisabeth Kubler Ross

Who likes consequences? I don't! Consequences need not be severe in order to be effective. Consequences need to be *appropriate* in order to be effective. A friend recently related that when two of her children were 35 minutes late walking home from school, she was very worried about them and her initial reaction was to be severe with the consequences. After dialoging with her children to determine the reason for their lateness and the extent of their regret, she determined that severe consequences were not required for this situation.

She asked them for suggestions and discovered that they would have punished themselves much more severely than she would have. In the end, the consequence was that they would not have the taco dinner that they had been looking forward to for their Cinco de Mayo celebration that night. Instead they had cereal and went to bed early. In the end, missing out on tacos was more effective than being grounded for a week. It is unnecessary for punishment to be extended, harsh, loud, mean, untimely, or unfair. However, parents should calmly administer fair consequences. Most importantly, this requires the giving of positive as well as negative consequences. Negative consequences must be balanced with positive rewards.

Tangible Rewards

A tangible reward is something real, substantial and sensible. In our family, money has always been the best tangible reward; however, special privileges are also given occasionally. The importance of this reward system is enormous. No matter what our age, we all enjoy tangible rewards, and they work. We, as adults, would not go to work and do what the boss asked if we didn't receive a tangible reward - the paycheck!

All too often parents see only the negative. Within every soul there is a rose. This rose embodies our good qualities planted at birth, growing amid the thorns of our faults. As parents, we have the duty to build our children by showing them their roses and not their thorns. Give positive rewards for your kid's roses.

Token Exchange

This is a system where you reward your child for *every single* positive thing they do or say. The reward can be anything from a tangible reward to a pat on the back or a word of praise. You could say something as simple as "That was a nice thing you just said to your sister." The little things you do or say may seem unimportant, but they actually show that you are constantly aware of the positive things they are doing.

Merits & Demerits

A good example of a fair consequence system is a merit/demerit program. This program is excellent for noticing and rewarding all the good behaviors as well as correcting the bad ones. We have used such a point system in our family. I believe it is a good example of fairness because it has stood the test of time. Our family has used it successfully for more than fifteen years, and our grandchildren now benefit from it. All five of our children, after having experienced the system, stand by it and use it in their families.

Keep a notebook with a page for each child. They record their own merits and demerits and are responsible for them. At the outset, explain to your children that you want to implement a new system to help you be more fair. Tell them you are doing this because you want to be sure that you never miss noticing the good things they do. Talk one on one with each child first and then together as a family. Describe the program as something that will help everyone in the family. Explain that you want to help them overcome any negative behaviors that may come up. Then, begin giving merits and demerits. Give rationale behind demerits and merits; in other words, explain yourself. Tell them how proud you are of accomplishments and good behavior as you give merits. And as you give demerits, be kind and loving but tell them that the particular behavior was unacceptable and deserving of demerits. This allows parents to remain calm, unemotional, and in control when giving consequences, since demerits punish the offense without belittling remarks or yelling.

Set aside a time every night, every week, or every two weeks to have a meeting, during which time you evaluate behavior and count merits and demerits. Reward them in a tangible way by totaling the merits minus the demerits and then determining a reward for the remaining merits. When our kids were young, each merit was worth a small amount, usually a penny. As teenagers, each merit was worth either a nickel or dime. This adds up to quite a nice amount, depending on how many merits you give. Start small. When we started, the young children didn't get more than 10 merits or demerits at a time. The amounts grew with their ages and accomplishments.

In essence, this takes the place of a meaningless allowance. Rather than blindly handing out money each week without attaching any accountability to your child's good or bad actions, their good behavior results in money. This also encourages dialogue between you and your teen.

If they are "in the hole" (have more demerits than merits), take away some privileges in a firm but loving way. NO grounding for days and weeks at a time. If you have a child who is hopelessly "in the hole," help them earn their way out by providing extra chores or opportunities that can result in merits. Normally merits are not given for doing chores. In our home, we expect that responsible teenagers can and should be expected to complete basic chores. However, merits should be given for maintaining a proper attitude while doing chores. Merits and demerits are based on behavior and attitude. Never say, "I'll give you a merit if you..." – it doesn't work that way. Give them merits for all the positive things they do: compliments received, report cards, kind deeds, and so on. Give demerits when their behavior is inappropriate. Be certain you don't misuse the program and notice only the bad behavior.

Once while visiting cousins in another state, the parent grounded one of the children for the entire week from the pool. The child had to sit outside the pool and watch the other cousins have a good time while getting reacquainted. The child's infraction was riding the bike without permission. This was an entirely inappropriate punishment because it was too long and severe, and it did not take into account the irreplaceable loss of camaraderie with cousins that would not be seen again for years. The parent and child could have agreed on a more appropriate consequence that could have satisfied the wrongdoing in a better way and at a more appropriate time.

In order to be effective, negative consequences must be given for an appropriate time period only. Too many parents give lengthy punishments due to their own anger and convenience. I know of a mother who gave a one-month grounding when she discovered her teenage daughter had been drinking. Raise your hand if you believe that grounding the daughter for a month will stop her from drinking. Not me! Let's get down to the real issues instead. It would have been better to discover why she was drinking through dialogue, love and concern, fair consequences, and if necessary, therapy.

Try to make consequences appropriate. In other words, don't take away a driver's license for being on the phone too long. Long, drawn out consequences are unreasonable. There is a father in Oklahoma whose sons regularly came home on time. The few times they were late, the father telephoned the police. This threat was always ever-present. Interestingly enough, these sons have chosen to depart from their father's values as they have grown to adulthood. The father's inappropriate consequence only taught them to dislike him and his values. He was equally ineffective when he would say, "As long as you live in my house, you will do what I say!" Force and coercion hinder us from making progress and building trust and friendship with our teens. Whether as adults or as teenagers, no one enjoys being forced.

Eye Contact

Always use eye contact when giving instructions or consequences; this helps ascertain whether or not you were heard. Did you receive a response? Before demanding perfection from your teenager, ask the question: Do we as adults follow instructions perfectly? Leave some allowances, be lenient, and understand that we all are imperfect.

Many times grounding is used as a consequence. This is overused and most often ineffective. When a child is troubled, the last thing they need is to be severely restricted. Talk to them. Try to understand their feelings. This shows your child that he or she is of the utmost importance to you, and everything else can wait. Let's be honest... why do we get so angry when we have to parent? That's what we are: parents.

Motivate

I know many parents who are so anxious for their sons to become Eagle Scouts that they make a rule that the son cannot drive until he gets his Eagle. There is no correlation between the two. These parents are punishing the boys in advance by threatening to not allow them to have their license.

Wouldn't it be better to make every effort to motivate and assist them with their Eagle Scout work, as well as in learning how to drive safely? Why shouldn't they achieve both? And when it comes right down to it, should they be forced to achieve an award? I think it is better to motivate than to coerce. If they are happily motivated, then there will be happy consequences.

A father once boasted that his children would learn the principle of obedience perfectly. I have felt sorry for his children, as they have grown up with rule upon rule and harsh consequences. I would venture to say that most adults would not put up with this treatment for very long, just as kids will not. His now-grown children have become deceitful and rebellious.

I knew a mother who complained because her twelve-year old son told lies. She said she had done everything and that her latest form of punishment was to use her husband's belt on him. I felt very sorry for the boy, and I wanted to tell the mother that the more she whipped him the better he would become at lying and not getting caught.

When kids lie, parents must look to themselves. Have you heard the saying,

"When you point a finger at someone, three fingers are point back at you?" In most instances, children feel like they cannot trust their parents enough to tell the truth. They fear the consequences of telling the truth. Instead, try to listen to their statements without confrontations. You can, and should, provide appropriate consequences later, after listening to them.

Teenagers can be motivated to solve their own problems if they are listened to. I know of a family who punishes their kids when their grades are not A's or B's. This has always been difficult for me to understand. I am interested in my children's academic achievement as well, but the last thing I would do is punish them if their grades dropped. My immediate concern would be to ask the question, "Why?" I would try to ascertain this information from my child through dialogue. Then I would proceed to find ways to motivate my child to want to improve, through offering assistance and possibly giving a tangible reward.

Rules

We have only a few specific rules in our home. Rules are oftentimes touted as being crucial in the family. In actuality, rules should be kept to a minimum and expectations should be maximized. For example, one of the rules in our home was that the kids were expected to call home by midnight so that we would know where the kids were, who they were with, and what they were planning to do. My husband and I didn't set out a long list of stringent rules for them to follow because we held high expectations for their behavior. Because we laid the groundwork early, we trusted them. We focused more on encouraging acceptable behavior and helping our teenagers make good decisions.

Through your example, your kids will know your values and expectations, and if you keep an open relationship they will strive to adhere to those values. Make certain that you keep rules to a minimum and that these rules will help you meet your children's needs.

Consequences

Consequences can be effective without being loud. Kids do not need to be yelled at. It is absolutely imperative that your voice and body language remain *neutral* and *mechanical*. You cannot let your child see that they have upset you. This puts them in control. Who's the parent, here, anyway?

Many parents view their job as a call to punish rather than a call to nurture. Dr. James Dobson tells one of my all-time favorite anecdotes in his film series entitled "Focus on the Family." He explains that police officers do not find it necessary to stand on the corner and yell at us when we speed; rather, they politely walk up to our car, smile, greet us, and say, "May I please see your driver's license?" They are very polite and courteous, and we, of course, are trembling with great fear. We are afraid of the consequences. We would not fear police officers yelling at us. It is simply consequences, properly administered, that are effective. When we draw the line and administer consequences, then we become effective. If we respond immediately the first time, they understand that line. If we wait for three occurrences then merely start yelling, they feel that leniency, or weakness in us. Children know where we draw our lines.

If you had a close friend who admitted some act of impropriety to you, you would not yell at them. It is more likely that you would express sorrow, comfort, reassurance, and understanding. You would probably not even give suggestions or advice. Do the same for your kids. Remember, your kids will probably punish themselves more than you ever could. They will feel remorseful for their wrongdoings. It is human nature that we are all quite aware of our flaws and shortcomings.

Angry confrontations never work. Some parents believe that they work because they see some initial results, but these are only short-term, and they do not build long-term relationships of trust and love. Confrontation teaches children to become deceptive when dealing with parents so that they do not have to endure any future confrontations.

There are many parents who not only spank small children but spank and hit their teenagers as well. Spanking, yelling, and hitting are not sensible consequences. Spanking children causes them to have less confidence and self-esteem. It also teaches them that violence is the best way to respond to difficult situations. Harsh punishment can also cause problems in adulthood, such as alcoholism, depression, and drug addiction. The American Academy of Pediatrics and the National Education Association condemn spanking. The National Committee for Prevention of Child Abuse says: "No child needs spanking."

Several years ago I attended a dog obedience school with Wrinkles, our Pug. The first caution our instructor gave was NEVER to hit your dog. I must admit there were times when I had done it. And I was always hurt when her little black, flat face would drop and she would turn away from me. I just didn't know how else to teach her. The teacher stressed this instruction throughout her class. She taught us that hitting completely destroys the dog's trust in you. Interestingly, in the same class she joked about the difficult times she had at home with her teenagers and that she at times resorted to corporal punishment with them. Hmmm..... never hit your dog, but it's O.K. to hit your kids??

CHAPTER 9
TEACH BY EXAMPLE

"Setting an example is not the
main means of influencing another,
it is the only means."
- Albert Einstein

No matter how much we SAY to our children, they learn the most from what we DO. Albert Schweitzer, a renowned French philosopher, physician, musician, humanitarian, philosopher, writer and Nobel Peace Prize winner, succinctly stated:

"There are only three ways
to teach a child.
The first is by example,
the second is by example,
and the third is by example."

Teens know our standards, values and beliefs from living with us and watching us. They will always absorb what we do more than what we say.

In an interview, First Lady Laura Bush said that she and her husband taught their daughters how to treat people by example. "They saw us with our friends. They saw how we treated each other," she explained. She also referred to a quote from James Baldwin about how children are never very good about listening to their elders, but they never fail to imitate them. Mrs. Bush said, "They saw the way we treated our parents. They saw the way our parents treated us."

I have a friend whose husband is a physician. He had very sloppy habits and did not keep his clothes and personal items picked up. He generally just dropped things on the floor. My friend, however, loved to pick up her things and keep the house clean and orderly. She explained to me that when her husband was a teenager, his mother consistently yelled at him and punished him for not keeping his room clean. She, on the other hand, had a mother who enjoyed housework and who showed her happiness as she worked by smiling and singing. Who was the most successful In teaching cleanliness? The answer is obvious: the mother that taught by example. Our children will be able to appreciate order and work if we ourselves have the proper attitude; we must acknowledge that our children are not our slaves, and neither are they our "property," as they were in earlier societies.

Be There

I have learned a secret that motivates kids to work around the home: work right along with them! Many times my son has invited me to his room to sit on his bed and talk to him as he cleans his room. Occasionally I will help him. But usually, he insists that I stay on the bed while he throws me his clothes and asks me to determine if they smell clean or dirty! So, once in a while, break from the mundane mold of, "Go clean your room," and instead say, "Let's do it together today; it will go faster." You might be surprised the next time you ask them to do a chore; they may respond more readily.

They're more likely to be enthused about housework if you are. Remember the mother who tried to teach her daughter how to keep her room clean by throwing everything into the yard? The saddest part of this story is that the mother gloated about her apparent success. Her daughter did keep the room clean in the future. However, this mother did not realize that their relationship was seriously marred because of the mother's lack of integrity.

Be Dependable

Be dependable and trustworthy—just as you would be with friends or co-workers. In this way, you will be teaching by example. Always make sure your kids know that you think of them as a priority. Follow through with your promises to pick them up on time. On the few occasions in my life when I have been left stranded because of miscommunication, I was deeply hurt and frustrated. Keep commitments with your children just as if they were with your employer or co-worker.

Be Creative

I want to share an example of two families that were trying to build spirituality in the home. The first family forced the children to study the scriptures at 5AM. On one occasion when I was visiting this family, the kids were unruly. I heard one parent shout, "Shut-up, we are studying the scriptures!" I believe the mean words and harsh feelings are what will be remembered from scripture study, not any spiritual experience.

I heard about the other parents through a speaker at church. They invite their children to attend scripture study. These same creative parents find ways to make the study enjoyable through intriguing dialogue and special treats. These parents are setting a positive example that will be easy for their children to want to follow.

Be a Teacher

Teach your teenagers how to live in our world; prepare them. Teach them to become assertive individuals. Don't confuse assertive with aggressive. Assertive means confident; aggressive means harsh, intense, and combative. Teach them by example how to engage in assertive conversations. The lack of simple conversational skills in many young people today is surprising. I am convinced that it is not common in most families to dialogue about how to be a good conversationalist. Teach them to ask questions, to show interest in others, and to be enthusiastic with others.

Don't forget to role-play! Too many of us—adults and teenagers alike—talk too much about ourselves and not enough about the other person and issues. By helping your children in this way, their personalities will begin to sparkle and they will be more ready to interact well with others.

Be an Example

I can't remember many specific words that my mother said to me when I was growing up. However, the things that *have* stayed with me are the things I saw her do. I observed her dry sense of humor when she spoke with others. She was thrifty and frugal. For example, once when she needed a couch for our living room and she had no money with which to purchase one, she very creatively set about to make one for almost nothing. She found an old door and painted it with black glossy paint. She got four screw-in legs, attached them to the door, and then added a back panel. Someone gave her a cot mattress and she covered it as well as two long pillows with leopard fabric. This beautiful couch was a conversation piece in our home for many years.

She was scrupulously honest in her dealings with others. This was evidenced by the things I saw her do, such as telling a store clerk that she had undercharged her. She also valued her health, and as a result disciplined herself by eating healthy food. We need to remember that example is sown mostly by the things we do, rather than by the words that we use.

CHAPTER 10
SELF-ESTEEM

*"We should seize every opportunity
to give encouragement...
it is oxygen to the soul."*
-George M. Adams

So much has been said and written about self-esteem. It is so essential to every human being. Self-esteem is our self-image; it is how we feel about ourselves. Do your teenagers think and feel positively or negatively about themselves? The more you feel positively about yourself, the higher your self-esteem is. The more you feel negatively about yourself, the lower your self-esteem is.

We need to help our teens discover their authentic self. If they appreciate themselves and the good qualities that they have, then they will care enough about themselves to make healthy and happy choices. Self-esteem can always be improved. We can accept ourselves even with our weaknesses, because everyone has them. We can explore and appreciate our own talents and we can love ourselves for being unique.

Give genuine compliments to your teenagers, especially about their character, talents and abilities, good actions, kindnesses—basically, all that you see them do that is positive. Remember, it is never too late to build self-esteem and to effect changes in behavior. Love and support your child through the wonderful change we refer to as adolescence.

A young person who has lots of self-esteem will stay away from relationships and activities that are inappropriate because they will want what is best for themselves. I once heard about a school system that implemented self-esteem classes rather than sex education, and it was successful. The district showed results: statistically, teenage pregnancies dropped after implementing the program.

When a teenager has a healthy self-esteem, it is easy to discuss all topics with them, including sexual ones. It becomes easy to emphasize that happiness comes when sexual activities occur at the proper time, and to emphasize the negatives that come when it is used at the wrong time. Discuss sexual topics just as often as you would other topics in the home. Talk about sex until all of their curiosity is satisfied and then they will not need to experiment. When their self-esteem is high enough, they will not need sexual intimacy to create a false sense of self-worth.

CHAPTER 11
TRADITIONS

*"I think togetherness is a very important
ingredient to family life. Cherish
your human connections –
your relationships with friends and family."*
-Barbara Bush

Traditions have held our country together for centuries; they can also hold families together. They can be as simple as a special family habit that you fall into, or as grandiose as making the most of birthdays and holidays. In our family, our children don't shut their bedroom doors. Our home is open. This may not be the case for all families, but the point is, establish traditions, and maintain them. So traditions can run from keeping doors open, to having a special plate for their birthday, decorating, playing, making a special breakfast, or taking them goodies at school. Have some traditional vacation spots for Spring Break, summer, or other vacations. I know one family who instituted "Children's Day," and celebrated just as they did for Mother's Day, Father's Day and Grandparent's Day.

Begin an after-school tradition. Make sure that at least one parent is always home after school to greet your child and help with homework. Spend time asking about your child's day. Have a big smile, warm hug and fun snack waiting when they walk in the door. Sit at the table with them. While they work on their homework, you could balance your checkbook, prepare a shopping list or go through the mail. Make it a fun time to be together.

One father used to take his children for Night Snow Walks in the winter. It was a terrific – and inexpensive - way for a father to spend time with his children. And his children will cherish the memory of those walks forever.

A favorite tradition in our family is talking at bedtime. Sometimes we get a little corny and sing a few songs or even tell nursery rhymes—we alternate between people and see who can tell the most rhymes by memory. Though nursery rhymes have all been but replaced with conversation and fun, we still enjoy gathering on the beds at night to enjoy spending time with one another. If the parents and children do not have a good relationship, this activity may seem ludicrous – but that doesn't mean you can't try it and see what happens. Topol said it perfectly: "Without traditions, our lives would be as shaky as the fiddler on the roof!"

MORE IDEAS

- ❦ Go to garage sales on Saturday mornings

- ❦ Go on a long family vacation: have children plan and carry out the vacation destinations, as well as fun car gifts to open along the way

- ❦ First day of school traditions. Buy them a special new outfit; take them out to a fancy dinner that night to discuss their first day of school, etc.

- ❦ Chaperone your kids' school dance, then take their group out after for pizza or ice cream

- ❦ Sleep in on the weekends

- ❦ Kids doing a Christmas stocking for parents

- ❦ Sleep in the backyard with the kids under the stars, or camp out in the living room with a pup tent—or make your own tent

- ❦ Service projects

❦ Read books together

❦ Find unique ways to celebrate holidays—have tacos on Cinco de Mayo, or a "green" meal on St. Patrick's Day (green mashed potatoes, beans, jello, etc.), or banana splits on April Fool's day

❦ Table gifts. This tradition began one year with all my children and their families around the dinner table. One daughter had secretly prepared gifts to present to everyone at the table; another daughter had done the same, as did my son. A humorous spirit of competition immediately surfaced, and each year, our big Christmas dinner has turned into a production... everyone trying to out-do everyone else with their silly "table gifts"

Dr. Steven R. Covey once discussed in a seminar three vital things parents should remember. He said that children learn first by the example of the parents. After they watch the example, they desire a relationship. Then, through the relationship comes the teaching. Teenagers don't want to hear what their parents have to say unless there is first an established relationship. So remember:

1) Example
2) Relationship
3) Teaching

Don't forget that love is the foundation for healthy children and teenagers. If they feel loved, then they won't be influenced as easily by media and other outside sources. We must tell and show our kids that we love them. Unconditional love, from a parent to a child, is an invaluable gift. It will allow them to take risks and know that if they fail, they will still be loved. No matter how busy life gets in these exciting, challenging, rewarding and meaningful years, don't forget to tell your teens, "I love you."